·GROWING UP IN·
Ancient Greece

CHRIS CHELEPI

Illustrated by
CHRIS MOLAN

Troll Associates

Library of Congress Cataloging-in-Publication Data

Chelepi, Chris.
    Growing up in ancient Greece / by Chris Chelepi; illustrated by
Chris Molan.
        p.   cm.
    Includes index.
    Summary: Describes daily life in ancient Greece, discussing life
in the city, life in the country, school, ceremonies and festivals,
food, and other aspects.
    ISBN 0-8167-2719-8 (lib. bdg.)   ISBN 0-8167-2720-1 (pbk.)
    1. Greece—Social life and customs—Juvenile literature.
[1. Greece—Social life and customs.] I. Molan, Chris, ill.
II. Title.
DF78.C53   1993
938—dc20   91-14852

Published by Troll Associates
© 1994 Eagle Books

Design by James Marks
Edited by Kate Woodhouse

Printed in the U.S.A.

10 9 8 7 6 5 4 3 2 1

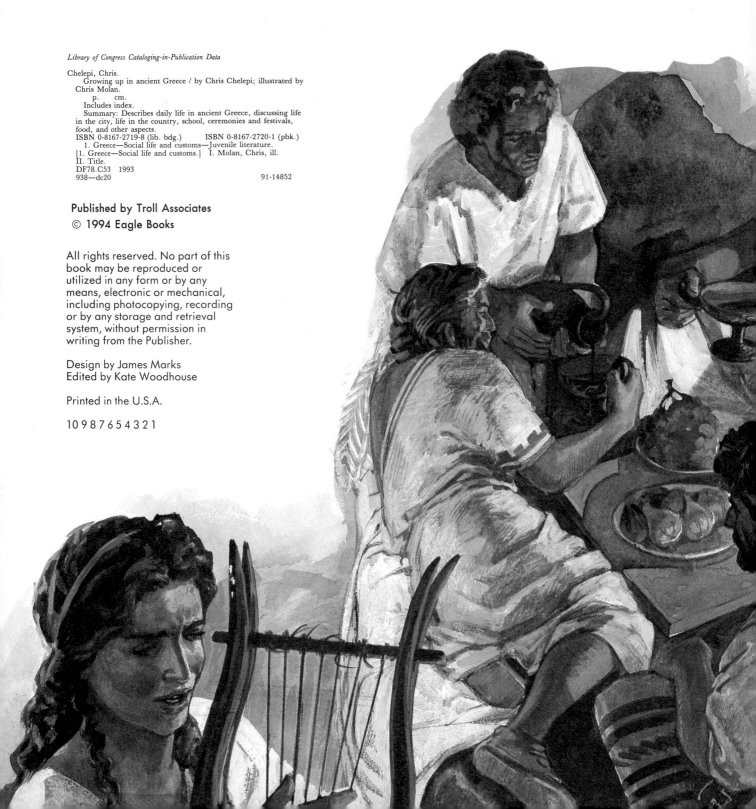

Contents

Introduction

In ancient times, Greece was made up of many city-states. It was not united into one country as it is today. A city-state usually consisted of a town and the villages and farmland around it. Some were bigger and more powerful than others. Two of the most famous city-states were Athens and Sparta.

Greece is a hot, dry, and mountainous country. The city-states tended to grow up in the valleys between the mountains. The land was not very fertile, but the ancient Greeks were able to grow much of their own food until the population grew too large for the land.

IONIAN SEA

EPIRUS

◄ Ancient Greece is well known for its varied and beautifully decorated pottery. Much of our knowledge of ancient Greece comes from paintings on pottery.

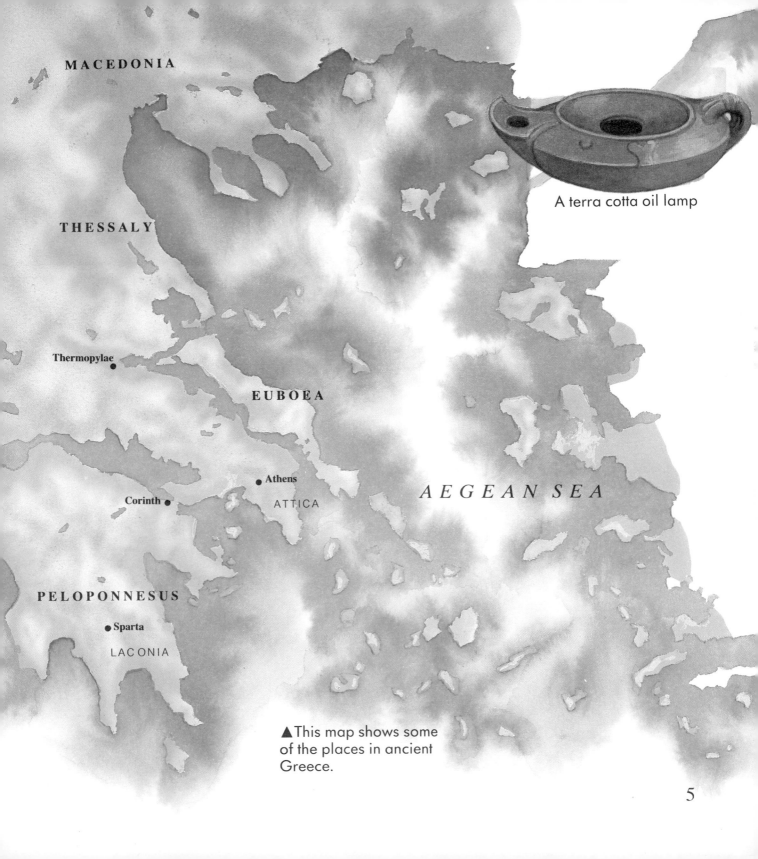

MACEDONIA

THESSALY

Thermopylae

EUBOEA

Athens
ATTICA

Corinth

AEGEAN SEA

PELOPONNESUS

Sparta
LACONIA

A terra cotta oil lamp

▲This map shows some of the places in ancient Greece.

5

Athens

Each city-state was built in much the same way. Above the city or town, there was a hill called the *acropolis*, which means "upper city." The Athenians and other ancient Greeks built temples to the gods to protect their city. These temples were usually built on the acropolis. At the center of the city was the *agora*, where people met one another to discuss important matters and where the market was held. Around the agora were houses.

▼Athens was the biggest and most beautiful city in ancient Greece. It would have looked much like this. Many people visit Athens today to see the marble buildings built by the ancient Greeks.

A few miles from the center of
Athens are the coast and the port of Piraeus.
Ships from other Greek ports, the islands around
Greece, and countries far away came here,
carrying goods to sell at the market. People from
other countries and other parts of Greece came to
live and work in Athens and Piraeus. There was
always work in one of the factories making shields
and spears. Piraeus was also a center for
shipbuilding.

Life in the country

The farmers of ancient Greece had to work hard all year, growing crops in their fields and tending their animals. Their children also worked hard.

From an early age boys and girls helped feed the animals in the farmyard, collect eggs from the hens, and milk the cows and goats. When children were seven or eight years old, they became shepherds or helped their fathers plow the fields. They sowed wheat and barley. They tied up bundles of ripe wheat and loaded them onto carts to take back to the farmhouse. In autumn, they gathered olives that had fallen to the ground.

If a family had food to spare, they took it to the market to sell to the townspeople. Rich families, who owned a great deal of land in the countryside, had slaves to do all the work for them while they lived in the town. Some slaves worked in silver mines or quarries owned by rich people. The work was very hard and many of the slaves died.

◄In summer, the children helped pick grapes and then trod them to make juice and vinegar. Children climbed trees to pick figs and almonds or knocked the fruit down with a stick.

9

Learning at home

When they were young, girls and boys played together in the women's part of the house. They had toys such as rattles, rocking horses, and dolls. Some families kept pet birds, dogs, and rabbits for the children.

By the time girls were seven or eight years old, they had a lot to do during the day. They learned how to spin and weave cloth, so they could help their mothers make clothes for the family. They had to learn how to run a home.

Most boys in rich families had their own slave, called a *pedagogue*. The slave's job was to look after the boy, take him to school, and sit with him in lessons to make sure he behaved. When they came home, the slave helped the boy with his homework.

The sons of poorer families would learn their father's craft. A potter would teach his son and, after many years of patient practice, a boy might become a master craftsman with his own workshop.

▼Athens was famous for the work of its potters, who were important craftsmen in ancient Greece. Many beautifully crafted and decorated vases from ancient Greece survive today.

Going to school

Very few girls went to school. Fathers thought it was better for a daughter to stay at home with her mother and learn how to be a good wife and run a home.

In Athens boys were required to learn a trade, but they did not have to go to school. Boys who did go to school learned to read and write. The poetry of Homer was one of the most important subjects they were taught. They learned much of his poetry by heart. The poems were about gods, heroes, and battles in faraway lands. Boys also learned to sing and play the flute or lyre, a kind of harp.

Boys left school when they were 14. Then they went to exercise every day at a gymnasium. There they met older, wiser men, and spent many hours talking together. They talked about science, mathematics, and the important questions of life.

▼The ancient Greeks loved sports. Boys learned to wrestle, sprint, and throw the discus and javelin.

Ceremonies and festivals

Many homes had an altar to the gods Zeus and Apollo. When the family prayed together, they offered a gift to the gods. It could be a cake, a bird, or a sheep.

When children were three years old, their father made a sacrifice to Zeus and Athena to thank them for letting his children survive life's dangerous illnesses. He also asked the gods to look after his children in the future.

Girls and boys older than three took part in the spring festival. The children were covered in wildflowers. The Greeks welcomed spring, and were happy to see the children and the flowers, because they stood for the future and were a sign that the gods were happy.

When girls were nine years old, they helped in the temple of Artemis. She was the goddess of wild animals. There was a story that a hunter once killed one of Artemis' bears, and the goddess became very angry because the hunter had not shown her due respect.

When a boy reached 18, he spent much of his time visiting holy places and temples. He learned how to make sacrifices and offerings to the gods.

◀These girls have dressed up to act out the story of Artemis and the hunter. One girl is the bear that was killed, another is the hunter who will show Artemis how sorry he is for the bear's death.

Clothes

The ancient Greeks got up when the sun rose. Getting dressed did not take long, because their clothes were simple. The girls and women wore a dress called a *peplos*. This was a loose garment, so it needed a belt tied around the waist. The boys wore a linen tunic that came down to their knees. The men wore longer tunics. In colder weather, men wore a long woolen cloak.

▼The clothes people wore were comfortable both for work and for coping with the very hot weather in Greece.

16

Everybody wore leather sandals, but farmers wore boots when they were working in the fields. Girls and boys had long hair, which they sometimes braided. Their fathers and grandfathers usually grew a beard, but kept their hair short. Their mothers kept their hair tied up in a bun, sometimes covered by a scarf.

It was the women's job to make the cloth for their family's clothes, whether they were rich or poor. The cloth did not need cutting or sewing, as the clothes were all made from a strip of material.

◀The edges of the clothes were sometimes decorated with a colored stripe or with a "key" pattern, like the one on the man's cloak.

Inside a house

However wealthy they were, the ancient Greeks built their houses with mud bricks. These bricks were made from a mixture of mud and straw, which was then shaped into bricks and left in the sun to dry.

Many of the wealthier homes had a passage that led from the front door to a courtyard with a well. The courtyard was open to the sky and around it were the rooms. Houses had small windows on the outside. Most of the air and sunlight came through the courtyard.

The biggest room was called the *andron*. This was where the men ate and had parties. Next to the andron was the kitchen, with a big fire in the middle of the room for cooking. When the women were not in the kitchen, they spent their day in another large room, where they did their spinning and weaving. The bathroom had a big basin for everyone to wash in. The bedrooms were usually upstairs.

►In town, some families had a workroom or a shop attached to their house. In the country, the animals were kept in one part of the house. There was also a room for keeping farm tools.

18

Shopping

Each town had a market around the agora, where people could buy almost anything they needed. Craftsmen worked and then laid out their wares for sale on the ground, in the shade of the long, cool marble buildings.

Slaves were sold at the market. You could inspect them and pick one you thought would be a good worker. There were also bankers in the agora, exchanging money for foreign merchants who wanted Greek money, so they could buy things in the market.

◄The market was divided into areas, so vegetables were sold in one part of the market, for example, and olive oil, fish, and meat were sold elsewhere.

The agora was an exciting place for children. There was the smell of perfumes and spices, the range of goods for sale, and people hurrying about.

Food

Most people started their day with a hot cereal. They usually had some bread and goat cheese in the middle of the day. Dinner might be fish and vegetables, followed by cheese, and grapes, figs, or almonds. Bread was the Greeks' main food, because there was no rice or potatoes.

The ancient Greeks ate red meat only on special occasions, such as a wedding or a religious festival. Then they sacrificed the animal, cooked it, and shared it among the family, their guests, and poorer people.

The women or slaves did the cooking, either over the fire or on a clay grill. They used an oven in the courtyard to bake bread. The potters made a wide variety of jugs, bowls, and cups to cook and eat with. For example, there was a type of wide-mouthed jug that was used for boiling water for soup or vegetables.

◄There are paintings on Greek vases of men having dinner parties, waited on by slaves and entertained by lyre-players. They would have eaten many different dishes, including perhaps fish, small birds such as thrushes and swallows, and yogurt in honey. Honey was used for sweetening, because the Greeks had no sugar.

23

Warriors

The Greek city-states often fought, usually over farming land or water. Sometimes they joined together to fight a foreign army. Learning to fight was an important part of a boy's education.

In Athens, when boys finished school they had two years' training to become soldiers. They were taught how to use shields and javelins, bows and arrows, and catapults. At the end of their first year, they were given a shield and a spear. There was a big parade in the town and each soldier promised to fight bravely for his people. In the second year, young soldiers continued their training in a fort on the city-state's borders.

▼Foot soldiers wore a breastplate made of stiffened linen covered with bronze plates. They also wore leg and foot armor attached to their sandals. Their bronze helmet had a horsehair plume.

▼The foot soldiers were an army's best fighters, with their double-edged swords and lances. Some soldiers fought with their hunting slings and bows as weapons.

If there was a war, every man under 60 had to go and fight. He had to be ready to go at a day's notice. Rich men who owned a horse joined the cavalry. At big religious festivals, young soldiers carried statues of the gods through the streets of the city.

Growing up in Sparta

Life in the city-state of Sparta was unlike the other city-states. The Spartans invaded and conquered the region of Laconia in the 12th century B.C. The people of Laconia became slaves, but the Spartans were always afraid they might rebel. So the Spartans trained their children to become brave warriors.

Any baby that was weak was left to die, and the others were brought up to be tough. When a boy was seven, he left home to live in a camp in the mountains, where he learned to be a soldier and an athlete. At 11, training became even harder. The boys wore only a cloak, had few baths, and slept on rough beds.

►Sparta was the only city-state where girls were treated as the equal of boys. The girls also had to train to be strong and fit. Girls and boys danced and raced together during festivals.

Spartans married when they were about 20, but even then the men continued to live by themselves in dormitories until they were 30. They had to sneak out at night to see their wives.

The Spartans showed their bravery in a famous battle, when about 300 Spartans defended the pass of Thermopylae against a much larger Persian army so that the rest of the army could escape.

Getting married

Except for the Spartans, the ancient Greeks thought a man should marry when he was about 30 years old. Usually the fathers of the bride and groom agreed on how much money or land they would give their children to help them in their new life. The bride could be as young as 13, and she might never have met her husband before the wedding. She may have been frightened at leaving her home and her parents.

Weddings were usually held during the month of Gamelion, at the beginning of the year. This was when the mother and father of the gods were married. The bride took a bath and dressed in her finest clothes to prepare for her husband's arrival.

When she reached her husband's house, the bride was welcomed by his mother. Everybody prayed to the gods that the newlyweds would have a long and happy marriage with many children.

Many of the writings, mathematics, and discoveries of the ancient Greeks are used today.

◄When it was dark, the groom arrived in a carriage with his best man, and took the bride to his house. All the guests would follow, singing hymns and holding lights.

Fact file

Science

Many aspects of science were discovered by the ancient Greeks. Hippocrates wrote about illnesses and how to cure them. He is known as the father of medicine. Doctors today take the Hippocratic Oath, promising to follow certain rules in treating the sick.

Other Greeks studied the stars. They calculated the length of the day and the year. Archimedes discovered that objects are heavier in air than in water. This is a basic law of physics. Many of the words scientists use today, like hydrogen and electricity, came originally from Greek.

Oratory

Oratory is the art of public speaking. Men showed their skill in arguing for their beliefs, in the market place, gymnasia, or courts. A few of the most famous orators were Lysias, Pericles, and Demosthenes.

Theater

The theater was popular in ancient Greece. Sophocles was a great playwright from Athens. *Antigone* and *Oedipus Rex* are two of his most famous tragedies. Sophocles died in 406 B.C. Another famous dramatist was Euripides. His best known play is *Medea*.

▲Actors in ancient Greece wore masks to show the type of character they were acting.

Writing

About 1000 B.C. the Greeks started trading directly with the Phoenicians. They saw many things there that were new to them, including writing. The Greeks took the Phoenician alphabet back with them to Greece.

▼A bronze statue of the goddess Athena.

Where the sounds were the same in both languages, the Greeks kept the letter that made that sound. They gave other sounds different shaped letters. In about 500 B.C. all of Greece started using one alphabet with 24 letters and writing from left to right and top to bottom. In Greece today people still use that same alphabet.

Philosophy

Philosophy was important to the ancient Greeks. Philosophy is the study of ideas and beliefs. One of the most famous philosophers was Socrates. He opened a school, where he was a popular teacher. One of his pupils, Plato, who was born in 427 B.C., kept a record of Socrates' discussions. Socrates believed that the human race could progress only if people kept to the law and did as they should for everybody's benefit. The Athenians felt he encouraged people to question their religious beliefs. To end this practice, which the Athenians considered dangerous, Socrates was forced to kill himself by drinking a poison called hemlock.

Index